First published in Great Britain in 1996 by
Brockhampton Press,
20 Bloomsbury Street,
London WC1B 3QA.
A member of the Hodder Headline Group.

This series of little gift books was made by Frances Banfield, Andrea P. A.
Belloli, Polly Boyd, Kate Brown, Stefano Carantini, Laurel Clark, Penny
Clarke, Clive Collins, Jack Cooper, Melanie Cumming, Nick Diggory,
John Dunne, Deborah Gill, David Goodman, Paul Gregory, Douglas Hall,
Lucinda Hawksley, Maureen Hill, Dicky Howett, Dennis Hovell, Nick
Hutchison, Douglas Ingram, Helen Johnson, C.M. Lee, Simon London, Irene
Lyford, John Maxwell, Patrick McCreeth, Morse Modaberi, Tara Neill, Sonya
Newland, Anne Newman, Grant Oliver, Ian Powling, Terry Price, Michelle
Rogers, Mike Seabrook, Nigel Soper, Karen Sullivan and Nick Wells.

ISBN 1 86019 4486

A copy of the CIP data is available from the
British Library upon request.

Produced for Brockhampton Press by Flame Tree Publishing,
a part of The Foundry Creative Media Company Limited,
The Long House, Antrobus Road, Chiswick W4 5HY.

Printed and bound in Italy by L.E.G.O. Spa.

The Funny Book of
FISHING

Selected by
Karen Sullivan

Cartoons by

Nick Diggory

BROCKHAMPTON PRESS

"Now today, I feel lucky!"

Last week I went fishing and all I got was a
sunburn, poison ivy and mosquito bites.
Leopold Fechtner

If today was a fish, I'd throw it back in.
Song

Visiting a prostitute is in the same league
as fishing or football as a leisure activity.
Hilary Kinnell

Each fisherman can wish,
That all the seas at every tide
Were his alone to fish.
*George Gascoigne, **A Farewell***

A canny young fisher named Fisher
Once fished on the edge of a fissure
A fish with a grin
Pulled the fisherman in —
Now they're fishing the fissure for Fisher.

Anonymous

Man: Are you fishing?
Fisherman: No, just drowning worms.

Angling may be said to be so like the mathematics,
that it can never be fully learnt.

Izaak Walton, **The Compleat Angler**

"Maggots, maggots, maggots!!
For God's sake can't you vary it a little?"

The wife of a fisherman was sitting on the bank of a stream reading a book while her husband fished. Someone came along and said, 'I need to speak to your husband. Can you tell me where he is?' 'Sure,' she replied. 'Just go up the stream that-a-way and look for the pole with the worm on both ends.'

A Treasury of Humour

To catch fish, think one step ahead. Big fish stay unhooked because foolish anglers can't outwit them. Let Nature remind you how to hunt — be animal cunning from the start. Wear drab-coloured clothes that blend with the background; wear nothing bright or flashy. Put tackle together away from the waterside and approach quietly; tread softly.

Ian Bell, **The Complete Fisherman**

*"That's just typical of you! 'A nice quiet fishing trip',
you said, and what happens? You run us aground!!!"*

*"I suppose you'll be using those
pathetic little maggots again, Harry."*

Man: How did you come to fall into the water?
Boy: I didn't come to fall into the water;
I came to fish.

As no man is born an artist, so no
man is born an angler.
*Izaak Walton, **The Compleat Angler***

The fish, still floating, do at random range,
And never rest; but evermore exchange
Their dwelling places, as the streams them carry.
*Edmund Spenser, **The Fairie Queene***

There's no taking trout with dry breeches.
Miguel de Cervantes

Some people are under the impression that all that is required to make a good fisherman is the ability to tell lies easily and without blushing; but this is a mistake. Mere bald fabrication is useless; the veriest tyro can manage that. It is in the circumstantial detail, the embellishing touches of probability, the general air of scrupulous — almost of pedantic — veracity, that the experienced angler is seen.

Jerome K. Jerome

First man: I tell you, it was that long.
I never saw a fish like that!
Second man: I believe you!

Angling is somewhat like poetry,
men are born to be so.
*Izaak Walton, **The Compleat Angler***

"Look Ben, isn't Daddy clever?
His first ever fishing trip and he's caught the
only mackerel in the Manchester Ship Canal."

"...and I caught this blighter by the nuclear power station."

Oh give me grace to catch a fish
So big that even I
When talking of it afterwards
May have no need to lie.
A fisherman's prayer

Fly-fishing may be a very pleasant
amusement; but angling or float fishing I can
only compare to a stick and a string, with a
worm at one end and a fool at the other.
Samuel Johnson

Float fishing is skilful and exciting.
Few sporting thrills compare to the heart-
throbbing moment your float quivers
with life as a fish bites your baited hook.
Ian Bell, **The Complete Fisherman**

Two experienced fishermen went ice-fishing. They chopped holes in the ice about twenty-five feet apart, put worms on their hooks, dropped their lines in the water, and got nary a nibble. This went on for several hours, but no luck. Mid-afternoon, a schoolboy arrived, walked confidently onto the ice and chopped his hole between those of the two men, and caught fish after fish.

The men were amazed, and finally one approached the boy and asked, 'Tell me young man, what's your secret.'

The boy replied, 'Mmmm, yummm mmms wmmm.'

'What's that?' asked the man. 'Say it again, please.'

The boy: 'Mmmm yummm mmms wmmm.'

The man: 'I am sorry. I just can't understand you. Would you speak a little more clearly?'

At that, the boy cupped his palms, spat a large amount of substance into them, and said clearly, 'Keep your worms warm.'

A Treasury of Humour

"Hey, look at that George – a knackered old boot!!"

Never feel self-conscious about crouching or crawling towards open bankside areas devoid of cover. Nobody will think you silly when you land the BIG fish others can't catch.

Ian Bell, **The Complete Fisherman**

For summer sickness, catch
An eel and let it cook.
Then — down the hatch!

Otomo Yakamochi, **Making Fun of a Thin Man**

We may say of angling, as Dr Boteler said of strawberries, 'Doubtless God could have made a better berry, but doubtless God never did;' and so, if I might be judge, God never did make a more calm, quiet, innocent recreation than angling.

Izaak Walton, **The Compleat Angler**

A fisherman went to fish a river, and having laid his nets across the stream he tied a stone to a long cord and beat the water on either side of the net, so as to drive the fish into the meshes. Someone who lived thereabouts saw him at work, and complained that he was stirring up mud and making the water unfit to drink. 'I'm sorry,' said the fisherman, 'but if I don't disturb the water I shall starve to death — and it will be your fault.'

Aesop's Fables, **The Fisherman**

First fisherman: Is this a good river for fish?
Second fisherman: Yes. It's so good that none of them were willing to leave it.

I love any discourse of rivers, and fish and fishing.
Izaak Walton, **The Compleat Angler**

First boy: Do fish grow fast?
Second boy: Sure. Every time my Dad mentions
the one that got away it grows another foot.

First man: While fishing, I spotted a whale.
Second man: Nonsense! Who ever heard
of a spotted whale.

To me heaven would be a big bull ring with
me holding two barrera seats and a trout
stream outside that no one else was allowed to
fish in and two lovely houses in the town; one
where I would have my wife and children and
be monogamous and love them truly and well
and the other where I would have my nine
beautiful mistresses on nine different floors.

Ernest Hemingway

*"Honestly Bob, it was all black
and shiny and bloody huge!!"*

23

Little boy: Hey Dad, what a great fish
you caught. Can I use it for bait?

No doubt the cod is a splendid swimmer, admirable
for swimming purposes but not for eating.

Oscar Wilde

Big fish are clever. They only live to grow
big by being smart. You have to get up
early in the morning to fool them.

Ian Bell, **The Complete Fisherman**

First man: Shame on you! A big man like
you catching poor helpless fish.
Second man: Well, if the fish would keep their
mouths shut, I wouldn't catch them.

A man walked into a fishmonger's and asked to buy six trout. 'Certainly sir,' said the fishmonger, selecting the trout. He was about to wrap them up when the man said: 'No! Please don't wrap them up yet. Can you just gently throw them to me one by one?'

'I can,' said the fishmonger. 'But why?'

'Well,' responded the man. 'I've been fishing all night and haven't caught anything. At least if you throw those trout to me and I catch them I can honestly say when I get home that I have caught six trout.'

The Huge Joke Book

And for winter fly-fishing it is as useful as an almanac out of date.

Izaak Walton, **The Compleat Angler**

"You were right Albert,
I am coming in handy aren't I?"

Given half-a-chance, some fish would eat anglers for breakfast — snap, crackle and pop!

*Ian Bell, **The Complete Fisherman***

"I think they're expecting you."

A Sunday School teacher, hard up for subjects
to talk about, was discussing with her class how
Noah might have spent his time on the Ark.
A girl volunteered, 'Maybe he went fishing.'
A boy countered, 'With only two worms?'

A Treasury of Humour

One, two, three, four, five,
Once I caught a fish alive,
Six, seven, eight, nine, ten,
Then I let him go again.
Why did you let him go?
Because it bit my finger so.
Which finger did it bite?
This little finger on the right.

Traditional nursery rhyme

Oh the slimy, squirmy, slithery eel!
He swallows your hook with malignant zeal,
He tangles your line and he gums your reel . . .
*Arthur Guiterman, **Song of Hate for Eels***

No man can lose what he never had.
*Izaak Walton, **The Compleat Angler***

No man can lose what he never had.

A man may fish with the worm
that hath eat of a king.
*William Shakespeare, **Hamlet***

Fred: The fishing today wasn't very good.
Claude: But I thought you'd had fifty bites?
Fred: So I did: one small fish and
forty-nine mosquitoes.
The Huge Joke Book

There are two kinds of fishermen: those who
fish for sport and those who catch something.
Leopold Fechtner

Sir Henry Wotton . . . was also a most dear lover,
and a frequent practiser of the art of angling;
of which he would say, 'It was an employment
for his idle time, which was not then idly spent.'
Izaak Walton, **The Compleat Angler**

First man: You have been watching me for
three hours. Why don't you try fishing yourself?
Second man: I haven't got the patience.

The only time a fisherman tells the truth
is when he calls another fisherman a liar.
Anonymous

When the wind is in the east,
'Tis neither good for man nor beast;
When the wind is in the north,
The skilful fisher goes not forth;
When the wind is in the south,
It blows the bait in the fishes' mouth;
When the wind is in the west,
Then 'tis at the very best.

Traditional

If fishing is a religion, fly-fishing is high church.

Tom Brokaw

Fish know we are hunters and keep an eye
on our latest baits, tackle and methods.
With more of us starting fishing for sport,
fish have extra practice avoiding our hooks.

Ian Bell, **The Complete Fisherman**

*"Crikey boys – we're going
to need a bigger boat!"*

First man: I just met a fisherman who hadn't had a
bite all day.
Second man: What did you do?
First man: I bit him.

Mistress Overdone: What's his offence?
Pompey: Groping for trouts in a peculiar river.
*William Shakespeare, **Measure For Measure***

When you're after eels for dinner,
Watch your step. Don't dive.
*Otomo Yakamochi, **Making Fun of a Thin Man***

There is a river in Macedon, and there is also
moreover a river in Monmouth . . . and there is
salmons in both.
*William Shakespeare, **Henry V***

'I am never taking my sister fishing again!'
sighed the small boy to his mother.
'Why not?' asked his mother. 'I know she's
only two but the water isn't very deep and you
can swim, so what's the problem?'
'She keeps eating all my maggots and worms.'
The Huge Joke Book

In communist society, where nobody has one
exclusive sphere of activity but each can become
accomplished in any branch he wishes, society
regulates the general production and thus makes it
possible for me to do one thing today and another
tomorrow, to hunt in the morning, fish in the
afternoon, rear cattle in the evening, criticize after
dinner, just as I have a mind, without ever becoming
hunter, fisherman, shepherd or critic.
Karl Marx

*"For goodness' sake George,
do you have to take it so damn seriously?!"*

Eschew the idle life,
Flee, flee from doing naught:
For never was there idle brain
But bred an idle thought.

George Turberville

The pleasant'st angling is to see the fish
Cut with her golden oars the silver stream,
And greedily devour the treacherous bait.

William Shakespeare, **Much Ado About Nothing**

Mr Jeremy stuck his pole into the mud and fastened his boat to it. Then he settled himself cross-legged and arranged his fishing tackle. He had the dearest little red float. His rod was a tough stalk of grass, his line was a fine long white horse-hair, and he tied a little wriggling worm at the end.

Beatrix Potter, **The Tale of Mr Jeremy Fisher**

*"You could be Widow bloody Twankey for all I care, Pal.
You still need a permit!!"*

Beware! Fish have ears!
Ian Bell, **The Complete Fisherman**

Although I can see him still,
The freckled man who goes
To a grey place on a hill
In grey Connemara clothes
At dawn to cast his flies.
W. B. Yeats, **The Fisherman**

A cook laid some live fish in a pan, and
started to fry them. As soon as they began
to feel the heat, one of them cried, 'There's
no enduring this!' So they all jumped into
the fire and were worse off than before.
Aesop's Fables, **The Fishes and the Frying-pan**

*"Oh Sydney, now you've got me out here,
don't go all quiet on me!!"*

There are as good fish in the sea
as ever came out of it.

I caught a tremendous fish
and held him beside the boat,
half out of water, with my hook
fast in a corner of his mouth.
He didn't fight.
He hadn't fought at all.
He hung a grunting weight
battered and venerable
and homely. Here and there
his brown skin hung in strips
like ancient wall-paper:
shapes like full-blown roses
stained and lost through age.
Elizabeth Bishop, **The Fish**

We fish, we fish, we merrily swim,
We care not for friend nor for foe.
Our fins are stout,
Our tails are out,
As through the seas we go . . .
Herman Melville, **We Fish**

The sea is not our friend. The sea is
neutral; it could offer us a big fish
and drown us — with the same wave!
Ian Bell, **The Complete Fisherman**

Fish (fly-replete, in depth of June,
Dawdling away their wat'ry noon)
Ponder deep wisdom, dark or clear,
Each secret fishy hope or fear.
Rupert Brooke, **Heaven**

WIDE

LOAD

*"Bye 'eck Bob, if you tickle it any more
it'll die laughing!"*

'Take my bait!' cried Hiawatha,
Down into the depths beneath him.
'Take my bait, O Sturgeon, Nahma!
Come up from below the water,
Let us see who is the stronger!'
And he dropped his line of cedar
Through the clear, transparent water,
Waited vainly for an answer,
Long sat waiting for an answer,
And repeating loud and louder,
'Take my bait, O King of Fishes!'

Henry Wadsworth Longfellow,
Hiawatha and the King of the Fishes

I am, Sir, a Brother of the Angle.

Izaak Walton, **The Compleat Angler**

In a bowl to sea went wise men three,
On a brilliant night in June:
They carried a net, and their hearts were set
On fishing up the moon.

Thomas Love Peacock, **The Wise Men of Gotham**

Sailing blossoms, silver fishes,
Paven pools as clear as air —
How a child wishes
To live down there!

Robert Louis Stevenson, **Looking-Glass River**

Swarms of minnows show their little heads,
Staying their wavy bodies 'gainst the streams,
To taste the luxury of sunny beams
Tempered with coolness. . . .

John Keats, **Minnows**

Dr Nute, retired after forty odd years of dentistry, is now free to ply the waters in the Molar II and drop a line where the fighting sunfish lie in wait. 'Open wide,' he says. 'This may sting a little bit. Okay. Now bite down.'

Garrison Keillor, **Lake Wobegon Days**

I went out to the hazel wood,
Because a fire was in my head,
And cut and peeled a hazel wand,
And hooked a berry to a thread,
And when white moths were on the wing,
And moth-like stars were flickering out,
I dropped the berry in a stream
And caught a little silver trout.

W. B. Yeats, **The Song of Wandering Aengus**

Simon Peter saith unto them, I go a-fishing. They say unto him, We also go with thee. They went forth, and entered into a ship immediately; and that night they caught nothing.

*John, **XXI: 3***

The perch swallows the grub-worm, the pickerel swallows the perch, and the fisherman swallows the pickerel; and so all the chinks in the scale of being are filled.

Henry David Thoreau

Somebody just back of you while you are fishing is as bad as someone looking over your shoulder while you write a letter to your girl.

Ernest Hemingway

"New float Ralph?"

The presence of noisy humans
scares away shy big fish.

*Ian Bell, **The Complete Fisherman***

"Alright, alright. I can't stand it any more - you can go!!"

The only reason I ever played golf in the first place
was to make enough money to hunt and fish.

Sam Snead

It is agreed by most men, that the eel is a most
dainty fish: but most men differ about their
breeding: some say they breed by generation as
other fish do, and others, that they breed of
mud; as rats and mice, and many other living
creatures are bred in Egypt, by the sun's heat,
when it shines upon the overflowing of the river
Nilus; or out of the putrefaction of the earth.

*Izaak Walton, **The Compleat Angler***

Like the gay fishes on the wave,
when the cold moon drinks the dew.

*William Blake, **Europe: A Prophecy***

Gonnnnne Fishing . . .

Oh! never fly conceals a hook,
Fish say, in the Eternal Brook . . .
Fat caterpillars drift around,
And Paradisal grubs are found;
Unfading moths, immortal flies,
And the worm that never dies.
Rupert Brooke, **Heaven**

In a warm day in summer I have taken
many a good eel by sniggling, and have
been much pleased with that sport.
Izaak Walton, **The Compleat Angler**

Only dead fish swim with the stream.
Anonymous

One unsuccessful fisherman to another: 'There are no fish in the sea: they're all up at Billingsgate.'

I know a deep and lonely pool — that's where
The great Kingfisher makes his sudden splash!
He has so many jewels in his plumes
That all we see is one blue lightning flash.
*W. H. Davies, **P is for Pool***

A garden saw I, ful of blosmy bowes,
Upon a river, in a grene mede,
Ther as that swetnesse evermore y-now is,
With floures whyte, blewe, yelowe, and rede;
And colde, well-stremes, no thing dede,
That swommen ful of smale fisshes lighte,
With finnes red and scales silver-bright.
*Geoffrey Chaucer, **The Parlement of Foules***

Time spent fishing is not
deducted from your account.

Anonymous

There are many people, even now, who have not
come to the right knowledge what a loach is, and
where he lives, and how to catch and pickle him.
And I will not tell them all about it, because if I did,
very likely there would be no loaches left ten or
twenty years after the appearance of this book.

*R. D. Blackmore, **Lorna Doone***

The axis of [the turbot's] eyes is not quite
parallel to the crooked mouth, and that is what
gives him his shrewd, malignant, I might say
underhanded look: he squints in quick motion.

*Günter Grass, **The Flounder***

*"That's it Rodney, toy with him for a while –
try to wear him out!"*

Canst thou draw out leviathan with an hook? or
his tongue with a cord which thou lettest down?
Canst thou put an hook into his nose? or
bore his jaw through with a thorn?

*Job, **LX: 1, 2***

Carp anglers use a very wide variety
of baits, including luncheon meat, banana,
boiled potatoes, and bread dough.

Old fishers never quit, they just change their tackle.

Anonymous

Some fishermen catch their best fish by the tale.

Anonymous

*"Okay Captain Birds Eye, stick it in the fridge.
The cat can eat it later..."*

*"Since I bought Daphne those flying lessons,
she lets me fish whenever I want.*

Acknowledgements:

The Publishers wish to thank everyone who gave permission to reproduce the quotes in this book. Every effort has been made to contact the copyright holders, but in the event that an oversight has occurred, the publishers would be delighted to rectify any omissions in future editions of this book. *A Treasury of Humor*, by Eric W. Johnson, published by Ivy Book, Ballantine Books © Eric W. Johnson, 1989; *Good News Study Bible*, published by Thomas Nelson, 1986, extracts reprinted with their kind permission; *Penguin Book of Japanese Verse*, translated by Geoffrey Bownas and Anthony Thwaite, published by Penguin 1964, and reprinted with their permission; *The Huge Joke Book* edited by Kevin Goldstein-Jackson, Ernest Ford and A. C. H. Newman, Elliott Right Way Books © A. C. H. Newman, Ernest Ford and Elliott Right Way Books; *The Tale of Jeremy Fisher*, Beatrix Potter, reprinted courtesy of Frederick Warne, a division of Penguin Book © Frederick Warne, renewed; *The Complete Fisherman* by Ian Ball, first published by Clarion MCMXCV, copyright © Ian Ball; *5000 One and Two Line Jokes*, compiled by Leopold Fechtner © Parker Publishing Company Inc., 1973; W. B. Yeats, from *The Song of Wander Aengus*, and *The Fisherman*, reprinted courtesy of A. P. Watt Ltd, on behalf of Anne and Michael Yeats, and taken from *The Collected Poems of W. B. Yeats*; P is for Pool, from *The Complete Poems of W. H. Davies*, published by Jonathan Cape, and reprinted by permission of the Executors of the W. H. Davies Estate; *Lake Wobegon Days*, by Garrison Keillor, reprinted courtesy of Faber & Faber and Viking Penguin.